the dictionary of flowers

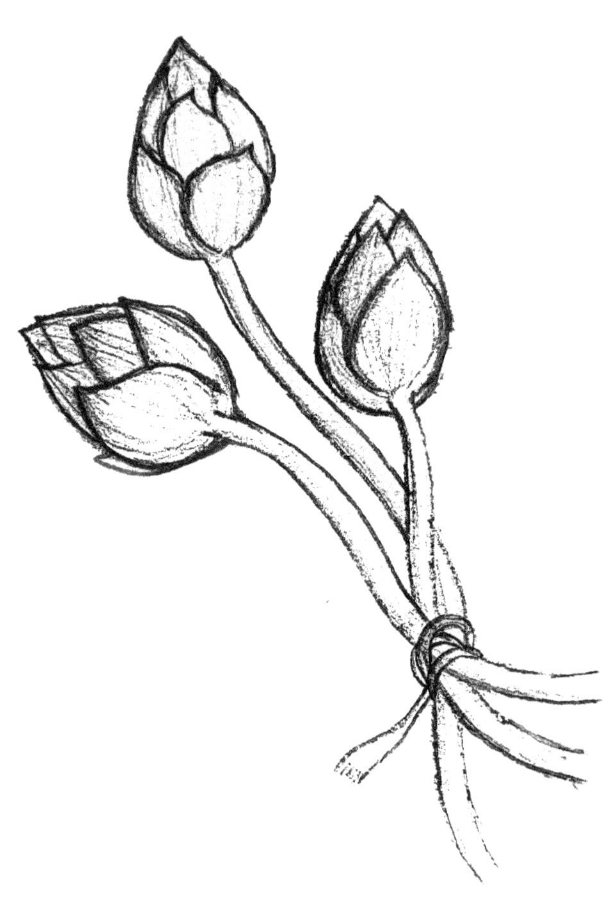

the dictionary of flowers

hariny ahana

First published in 2021 by Cinnamon Teal Publishing.

Hariny Ahana asserts the moral right to be identified
as the author of this book.

Illustrations by Rohit Bhasi
Design by Alice Woodward

ISBN: 978-1-0684704-1-7

Contents

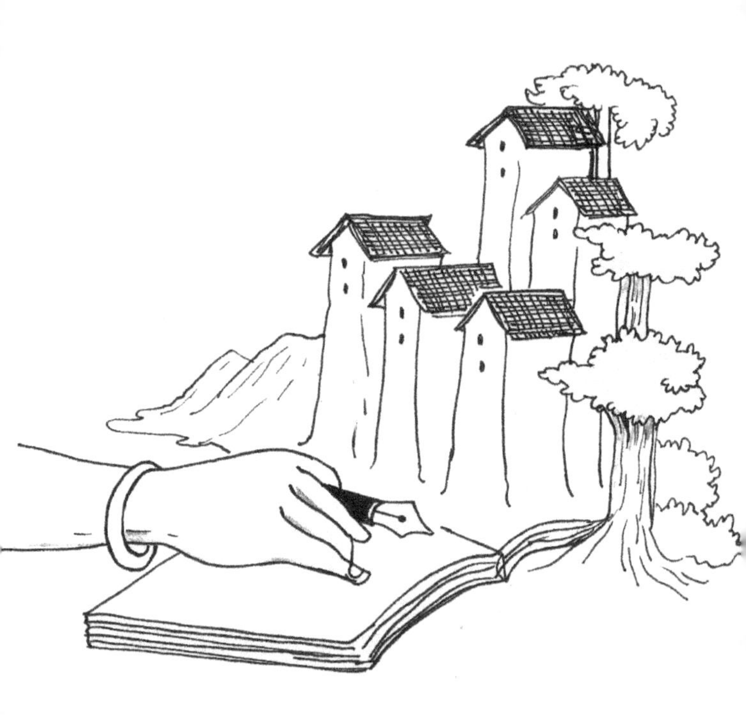

Foreword

Imagine a poet in a state of lockdown within a university hall,
feeling her way beyond the routine of impersonal institutions
using language to guide her to the natural world as emancipation.
The 21 vignettes in *the dictionary of flowers* take the violence
and cacophony of Delhi, the hard and fast rules it imposes on
women's bodies and minds, and reframe them as a longing for
a warmer South Indian home, a place where even the street
lights, landing on some cheap plastic chairs in a side alley café,
offer the promise of belonging.

In these prose poems, the pressure of homesickness expands into
a dream of escape. Everyday objects hold memories, but are also
transformed into possible future lives. The poet knows she is in
a holding pattern and pushes against the bars of the cage.

She is unafraid for whatever might come once she breaks out
and sets herself on a new path. Where will she arrive? The most
evocative writing asks us to imagine what a character, in their
world, might do on her journey. These pages are bursting with
the possibilities of words, though the writer always holds herself
in check. Through careful imagery and vivid phrasing, she asks us
to consider with her: *What happens to the words within, the ones
the world never gets to see?*

Such poetic craft – the idea that less is more, that mixing tongues as tastes is political – underpins what this first collection reveals: a confident new voice that dares us to acknowledge the latent trauma of the everyday, and the possibility of new worlds coming into being in fresh, surprising, and longed for ways.

You hold in your hand the work of a poet we will see much more of in the coming years. This is her beginning: it's an honour to share in it.

~ Preti Taneja, author of *We That Are Young* and *Aftermath*

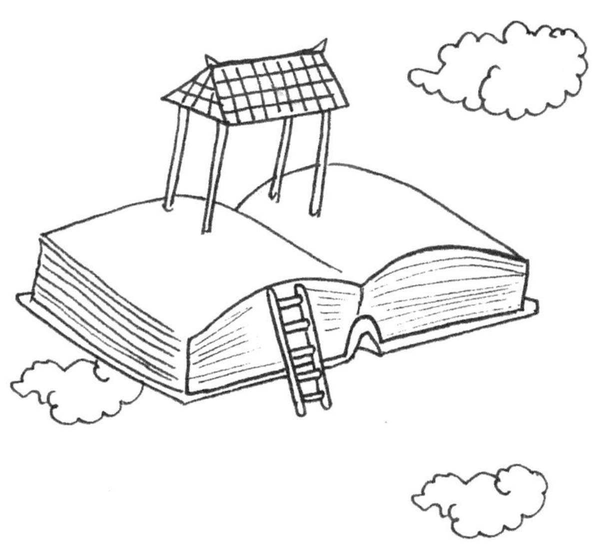

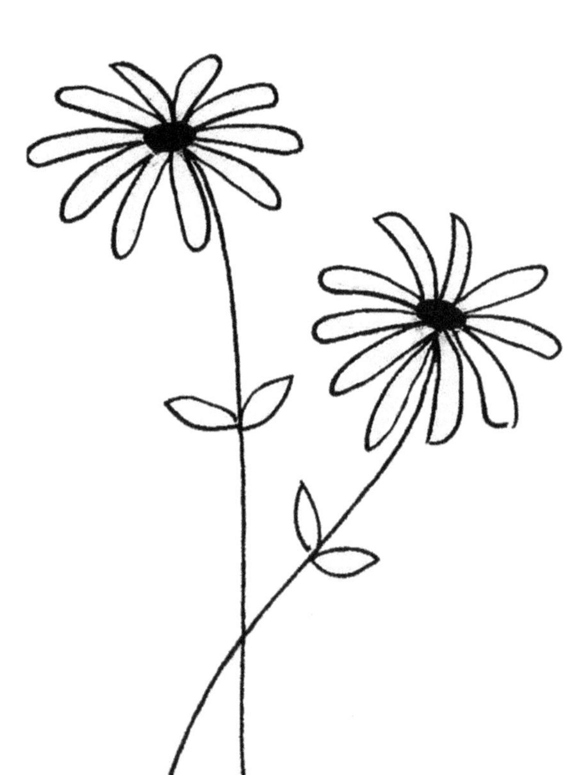

the dictionary of flowers

Two springs and three twilights ago,
I met a boy who collected jars of wild honey
from within cavities of trees.

He trailed after memories
of susurrating leaves and thought of people
wearing flowers, whose nectar
his fingers were often sticky with.

He grouped them in his mind,
in bouquets of blossoms and buds,
smiling in the company of others,
quivering on his own.

I asked him why.
Why do you choose different flowers
each time you meet another person?
He looked up, surprised
I would question something
so habitual to him,

things he had been doing for years.
Yet nobody had ever wondered
about the many reasons
for his tiny dictionary of flowers.

He sighed.
Thought for a while,
shaping and giving
words to the customs he had formed.

He gave orchids to the ones
whose thoughts and minds
still remained a void of mystery,
drew him closer with an enigmatic caress
but revealed not a single reason
behind their abundant riddles.
Puzzling him, thrilling him,
with secrets
in their purple whorls.

Carnations, he felt, were accentuators
in an existing scene of beauty
and looked lost when left alone.
Their presence filled him up with a distance
from himself. He often gave bunches
of these flowers in light and differing shades
to people towards whom he felt obliged to give
a little something
but did not feel any particular warmth for.

Multi-shaded chrysanthemums
for everyone who took him back
to his younger days when he
ran across wet stone floors
in the temple next to his house,

going on expeditions for his mother
who waited for those flowers.

He strung jasmine for those
who had known him forever
and could never let him go.

Blooms of lilac for children
who sought him out, bringing with them
the lost echoes of his childhood,
evenings in parks with damp grass,
his sister gathering droopy petalled flowers
as she waited for him to catch up.

Roses! I said, *They should hold
their usual significance*. He nodded.
Then told me about the hierarchy of his roses.

White ones for a coffee, new dates
at places calm and cool when expectations
still ran low. *Yellows are in the middle*, he said.
Not too bold, nor do they fade into the background.
Yellow was subtle and elegant,
meant for ostentatious dinners and first dances.
Syncing hearts, but not too much.

Red, he whispered. Red roses reminded him
of his first crush. When he had never dared to get close
instead standing far away, clutching colourful postcards.
Red was deep and wanted to be seen.
Red reminded him of her first shade of lipstick.

The romance he knew so well but never had.
Red was rare. Red was scary.

I don't think I've ever given a red, he confessed.

Sunflowers.
His face softened. His smile was huge,
trailing behind thoughts of freedom,
even if it was within the confines of his own mind.
Sunflowers were his favourite.
He gave them to those he adored.
The people who still gathered around,
even when he couldn't muster enough joy
—the sunshine he looked towards.

Often, those who received his daisies
wondered why they didn't get
a more colourful shade,
and the ones who waited in despair
for his roses were left confused
and longing for more
when he gave them a single sunflower.

You will get an assortment,
not just one, he told me.
Wiping clean his sticky fingers
that constantly smelled of honey,
he slipped into his garden
to tie up the perfect bouquet for me.

I didn't want to know, back then,
what my flowers would be.

Before I stood up to leave,
I took out a few pink lotuses
pale and full of dew,
from the early waters of the temple pond,
tied them together with frayed ribbons
and left them beside the leaves
on his little porch.

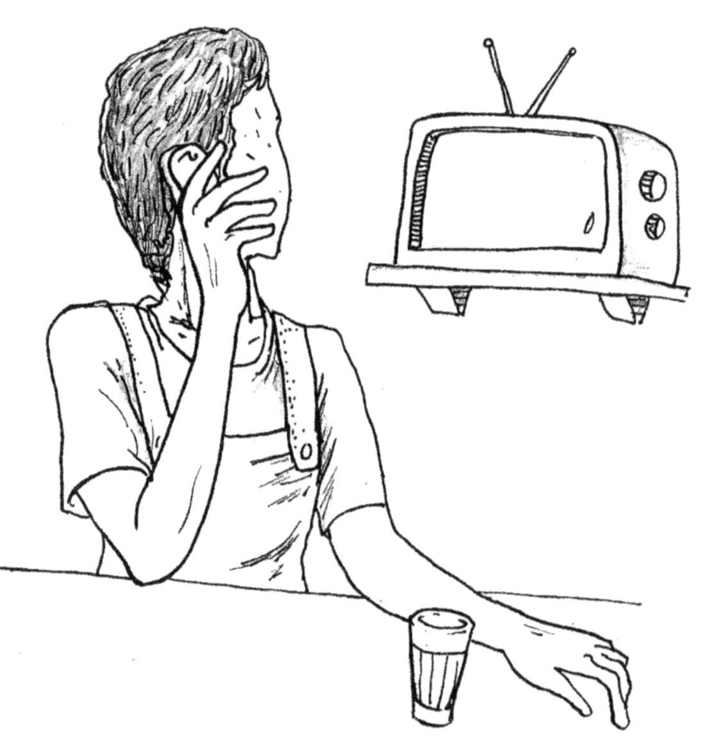

Castles in the Air

He builds castles in the air
on rainy days when he looks up at the sky,
wondering if the falling drops trace a way back home.
Sunshine and rainbows are no better;
the castles with twirling flowers and spring ponds
cave in and grow darker,
until they are no more than a mound of purple mud
frozen within a barred cage.
On days like today he dreams
of faraway mountains shaded a violet-gray,
a faded brown house standing alone
in the middle of a place where breaths echoed
and snow was melted in salamander stoves.
He thinks of his giggling sisters by the river,
hands filled with bangles of glittered plastic.
His mother, who fastens huge golden rings through her ears
and adds a flaming orange petal to it,
lights the lamps—
a tender twinkling gold,
one last time before the night.

He wakes up soaked in sweat,
borders and miles away,
to a plate of broken biscuits and cold rotis,
a twice worn shirt with
ten rupees for the bus.

He thinks of the aisles left to clean
and his friends with books back home.
Then he begins to dream with glazed eyes
of castles in the air
from which he finds no respite.

Hayati

you walk barefoot
you wear silks bordered with gold
and anklets of silver and rose
you cross your legs and keep away from the armrests
you sit next to books you are held back from
and look at me
silently asking
if I can do something about it.

you stand tall
you hide yourself behind shawls of lace
stitch tiny daisies onto your pants
and sleeves
you fluff the pillows and walk out
like nobody is at fault
I ask you to talk to me
you reply with a stare that says
I am far and gone

you part your hair in the middle
let it grow wild
long past your brown shoulders and
robes of creamy ice

you wear diamond rings
paint your lips
to run naked in young cotton fields
you look back at me with shining eyes
and a smile that is buried in secrets and many lies

you are young and free
at least you should have been
you are covered in cloaks you despise
fettered in chains with glitter and stones
you live between hands and words
that strike and touch you with no fear
you are too scared to look up
at me
and realise we are not so different
you and I

you live in worlds of snow
with a handful of pearls
you hide your wrists under strings of cloth
similar to your worn and tender breasts
you are the only one
that knows me
every inch and breadth
you trace a line on my cheek
whisper my name
wait and wait for me to
break your wounded cage

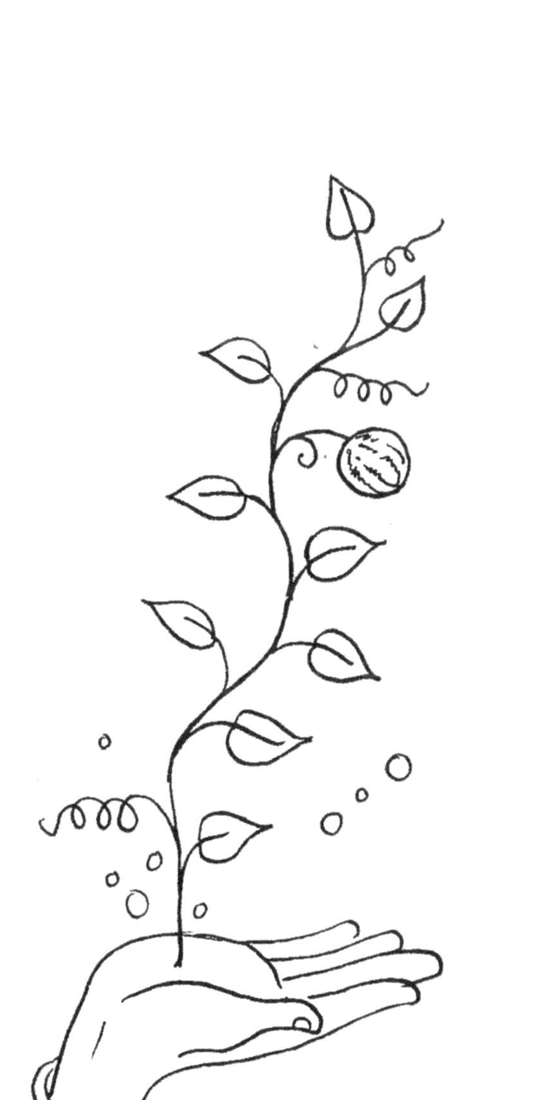

The Days the Melons Grow

The days the melons grow
under dripping heat and half-baked rays
nights steeped in an August glow.

Her eyes are fenced with kohl curves.
The shades of red, too bright
even as they slowly slip from her bitten lips.
The long braid of her hair
twines its wildness
with blooms of sultry jasmine
pressed with marigolds.

A worn saree
faded with rivers and bursts of pink
shrouds her frame,
revealing the whitened flesh
on her hungry waist.
It cocoons her close
until it is ripped with too much force
by hands that devour and a glance
that does not forgive.

The days the melons grow
the shiver in the air
bears deep through her eroded bones.
She shrinks herself in,

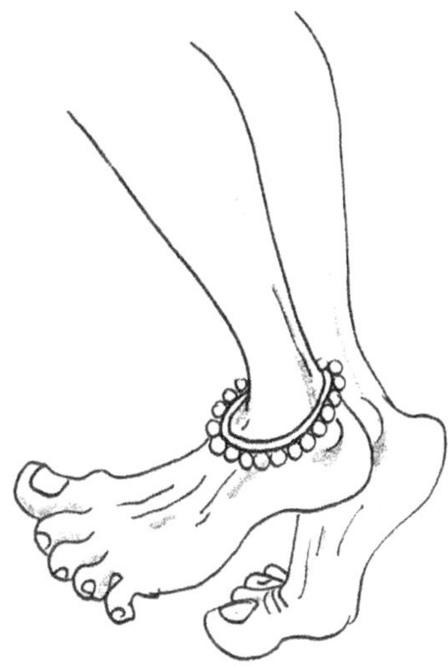

away from the gurgle of crowds
and words that lather her
with grey tears and a lame heart.

Stunting flagrant thoughts
tortured till dawn
the stains on her carpet
are too many and too stubborn
to simply wash away
with soap and the promise of a new day.

The days the melons grow
she dreams of people's eyes
like they are a pair of moving shutters
she can't get away from.
Little pools of diamonds
sizing and branding her
wherever she walks.

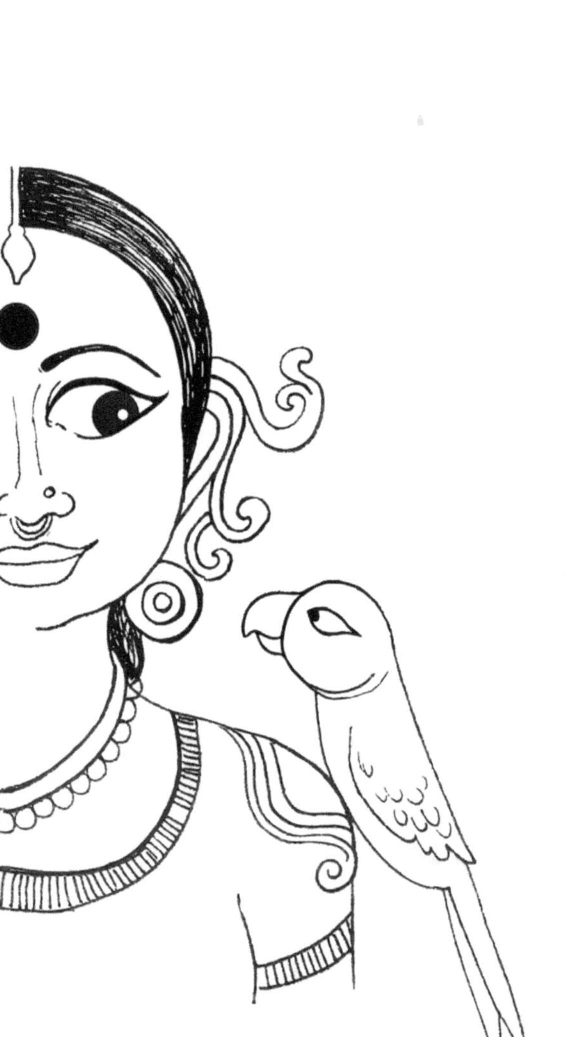

The Fish-Eyed Queen

I remember her today
as the skies shudder open
purging rain and light
over her temple towers.
Arranged in a distant square.
Lasting shapes in the storm and dark.

She stays silent in her shrine.
Dormant to prayers
from gruff voices
that promise her the world,
weeping tears and easy wealth
but shackling her sisters,
less powerful than her.

My thoughts sink to the time
when she ruled over our lands,
renegades and pilgrim hearts.
Creating a city and legacy
blinding in their glory,
maternal at heart.

Some say she slowly froze,
behind garlands of maroon and red
robed in the richest green silks,
bathed in milk and roses freshly picked.

Hidden by shadows
of the millions that suckled her warmth.

Others like to believe
that she still watches the streets
and stalls. Fierce as we were told.
But lonely under violent new norms.
Walking amongst women
with futures inescapable and torn.

I look at you from afar
wondering what it all meant.
The stories of the Mother Queen
who stood guard at the centre,
vowing to protect us all.
Now made beautiful
to fit the verses of a fabled myth
forever inscribed in the pages
of a softly forgotten age.

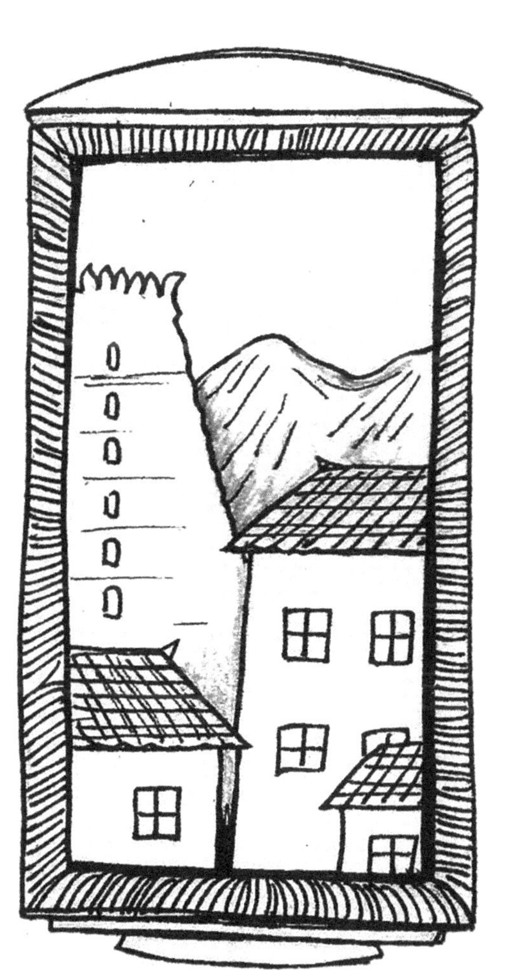

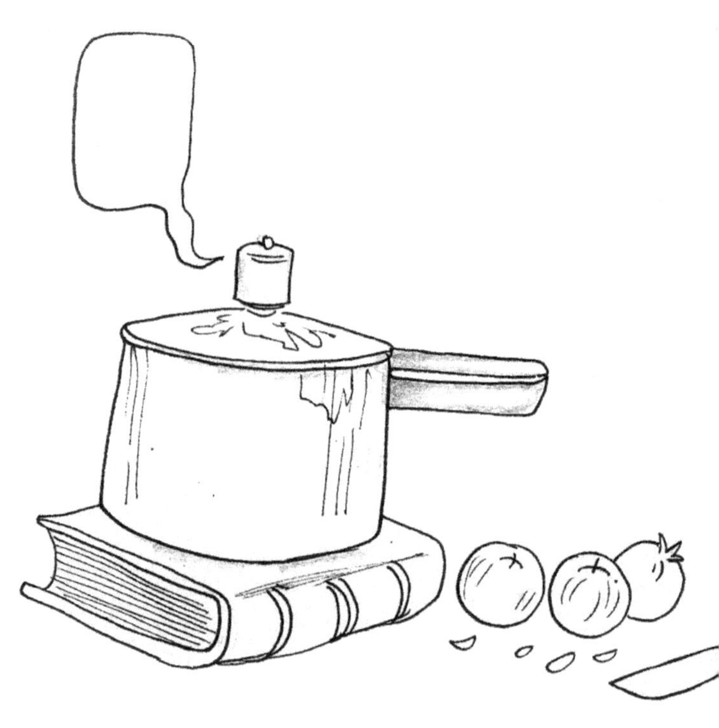

Cooking Scars

I got my first kitchen scar a few weeks ago.

The stove was on. I was pressing the tomatoes with a ladle,
squeezing them against the floor of the pan. Letting the gravy soak
in everything it could. A sudden whirl of steam rushed past my
hands and my fingers brushed against the sides of the hot saucepan.

I didn't feel anything right away.

Soon the chillies were cut and tossed in with the final spices and
some salt. I felt a slow burn on my hands. I walked to the window
and tugged the curtains out of my way. Under the light of the fading
sun, I watched a red scar slowly creep into the back of my fingertips.

I have had bruises that caused more pain and left deeper scars.
And kitchen scars aren't unusual nowadays. It's something to
be expected in the present age. When everyone has learnt to
take to the stoves and ladles, chuffed with this *new* form of art.
Ignoring memories of the past when hunched figures spent hours
in the kitchen, day after day, without having to ask.

That evening, when the aroma of bubbling tomatoes and chopped
onions filled the house, I only thought of one thing.

The ringlets and curves of red, brown, and black that dot the
palms and wrists of my mother, her mother, and hers.

Saturday

It is another day, and I immediately long to be home.

The walls around me are bare. The white paint is peeling off
in layers.
The falling cement scatters in the morning air, muddying my view
of the rest of the room.
A room in which there is nothing much to really see or discern.

Everything is quiet. Everything is still.
Not the Saturdays I grew up with.

I close my eyes again and imagine myself a thousand miles away,
succumbing to the pull of the powerful seas down south.

I pretend that the walls around me aren't a shade of sickly white.

They slowly change until they are strong and painted in shades of
flowing cream. Until they resemble the walls I have always known.
I lean over and touch the floor. Black-veined marble, cool against
my fingertips.

The curtains are printed with dark red and golden leaves,
shimmering under the sun, fluttering in patterns against my desk.
There is a group of morning doves idling by the windows at
the back.

I am swathed in my summer blanket, smelling of lavender soap.
I know if I reach out a hand, I'll be able to feel the worn spines
and covers of scattered novels. Books that always lie open beside
me as I sleep.

And any moment now, I'll be able to smell the spicy onions and
tomatoes cooking on the stove. A mild sound of vessels clashing
against each other. The ladle scraping against the pan. Shifting the
onions. Pressing the tomatoes. Making sure that everything gets
their needed warmth.

The ripping of a paper bag from the bakery.

I remember the small bakery down the road where we have
been buying bread every weekend for the past twenty years.
We consider their bread the best in town. Soft and rich, baked
with all my memories of cosy Saturdays at home.

My mother takes out fresh loaves and places them on the pan
in groups of three. She pours her homemade ghee on the tiny
squares and sides of the bread. When they are soaked and
toasted enough, she arranges the slices for everyone on different
plates. Mine is circular and silver in colour with exactly six slices
of bread. Heavily soaked in ghee, sometimes toasted after a dip
in a bowl of beaten eggs. The spiciest of the tomatoes and onions
are always left to me. Placing them within large chunks of torn
bread, I roll them together before taking a bite.

But for now, I am still in bed. The blanket is still tightly wound.
And my eyes are closed. The walls around me are painted with
cracks of falling cement. Breakfast will be a cup of cold and

watery coffee from the night before. And tomorrow is another day I'll have to walk into college and laugh with people I no longer relate to.

For now, my eyes are still closed. I imagine that my breakfast waits warm and ready on a round silver plate. And that the walls around me are strong and spotless.

I think back to the home that is a million steps away. A home that stays put and clasps tight, all the days and nights we spent together as a family of four –
lonely but content
broken but fleetingly happy

on a warm Saturday morning.

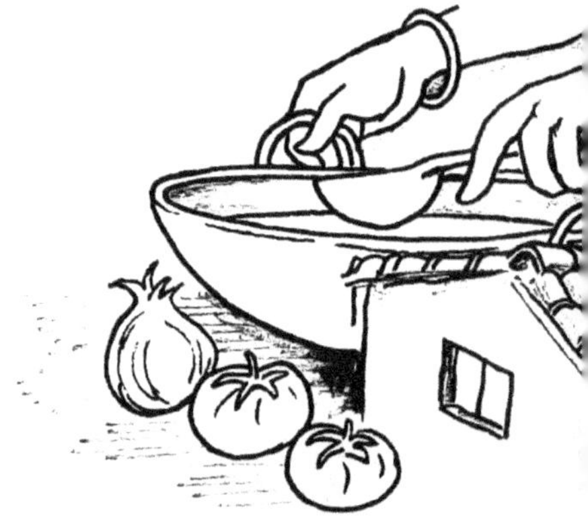

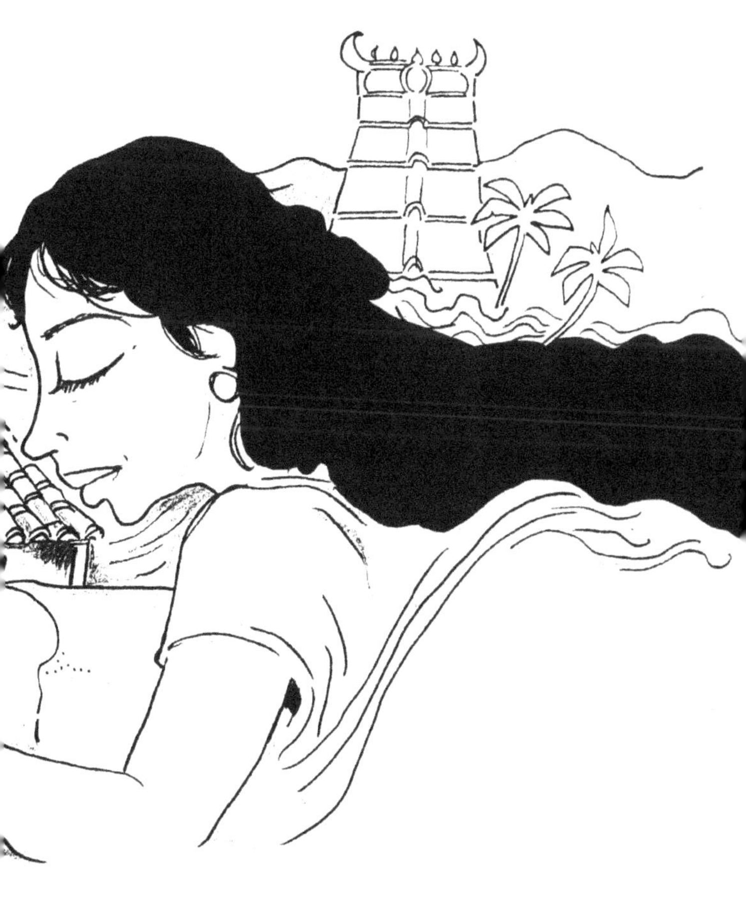

Charred

Too many scars trace their way
down the dark weaves of her body.
Scars that force one to pause,
to conceal a gasp of shock.
That a face so filled with vigour and warmth
houses stories of such traumatic loss.

The charred shapes of circles and slashes
show the patterns where long tongues of flame
once danced their way across the skin
of her upper arms, which she always covers with a shawl,
and the part of her back that's always hidden
by the screen of her falling hair.

Tiny ringlets of black and cream
on her fingers and wrist
from the flames of her cooking vegetables
and knives filled with swollen peels.
The scaled roughness on her toes and hands
hardened by the water of burning detergents
and sponges filled with lemon and soap.

Sometimes when she stands behind me,
pouring a handful of oil into my hair,
I feel the softness of her stomach
pressing against my back.

I think of the scar right there
concealed behind her clean cotton clothes.
A small curve I shiver to touch.
Gently arching and shaped like a slow hook,
brings back memories of hospital lights
and green gowns she hated getting into.

Stained sarees and bedroom sheets.
Spots of blood she kept washing
before anyone else could see.
Blood that only bled.
Never pausing to take a breath.
Hospital lights and green gowns.

We have to stop the blood,
they told me. Stop the blood before it
could drain away all the life she held.
The only time I saw her shake and shudder
clutching my hand like I was the mother.
Pleading and wishing with everything in her eyes
to halt the pain.
To harness the body that had
slipped out of her control.

The place she once gave a heartbeat
and felt a life kick,
gnarled into a limp scar

frozen with memories of wrath.

Suitcase

I have a dark blue suitcase hidden under my bed, a place from where it is always visible but not quite reachable.

Most days it is very heavy; others, not so much. The edges are stained with the patterns of wet grass and the top has a large circular coffee stain.

The suitcase remains shut except on rare occasions when I force it open to drop in another relic to keep safe.

The last time I checked up on it, which was almost half a year ago, there were quite a few things inside. Things I have forgotten about and would probably forget altogether if they weren't contained within this suitcase.

At the very top there is a piece of sea glass. The curves are smooth and the sunlight often used to reflect the mint green cracks on the glass before I shut it away. It was gifted to me by a friend who loved the beach, who I no longer speak with. Many days after both of us forgot why it was with me, I still held the sea glass tight. Pressing it against my palm to take me away to a place with sunlit waves and fresh winds, where it was easier to breathe.

Beneath it are a couple of old photo albums with loose pictures that keep falling from between its pages. They hold moments

from the lives of all my brothers. As babies and overgrown
toddlers. Wearing my frocks and bands, with pods of jasmine
strung together and arranged on their tiny, hairless heads.

There are a lot of hardcover novels. More novels than I'd need
at any given time or be able to read. They are crammed tightly
together with clean and intact pages, waiting quietly, to erase
my irrational fear that one day I'll have read all the books I own
and not have any escape left to turn to.

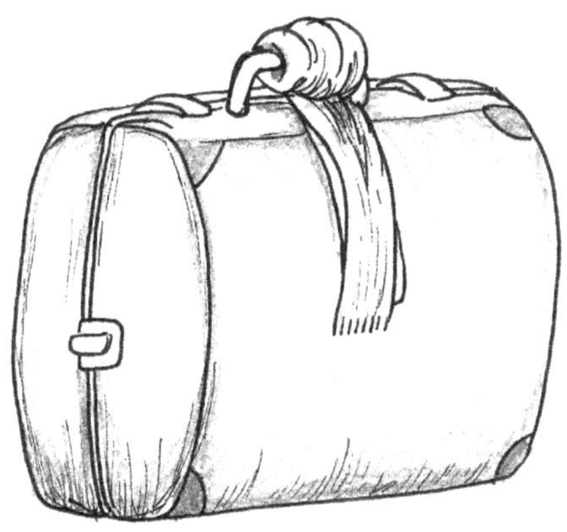

Three sarees are pressed between the books. A bright green
that glows more in the dark, purple silks mixed with gold, and
a deep soft brown with borders of burnt yellow—these sarees
weren't worn as often as they should have been. Taken out during
festival days or times when we washed our hair, pinned strings of
bright flowers, applied kohl to the eyes and walked to the temple
at the centre.

There are old greeting cards underneath. Handwritten and
stencilled by a summer friend when I turned sixteen.

And letters. Plenty of scribbled letters with pencil
drawings from an ex I sometimes struggle to remember.
The letters he wrote to me in his college notes. The bookmarks
of dancing penguins he painted all night to fit within the pages
of my books, so that when I did what I loved most, all I thought
of was him.

Still intact glass bottles decorated with hearts and confetti.
And the one t-shirt of his I decided to keep because it had four
small roses and a cocoon of leaves printed on the front and back.

A journal I once bought because it had rainbow flowers on its
cover but abandoned after the first five pages. Pages that are now
limp with a half-finished story about an artist who could only
paint shards from the future and nothing else.

A pair of trousers stitched with a patchwork of patterns.
Patterns of dots and stripes of colour that came from the home
of a young woman selling cheap clothes in the bazaars of the
pink city.

A large bookmark with an intricate painting of a royal
horse, which I picked up from the crumbling stones of
my favourite castle.

And tall wood tumblers with tiny dessert spoons in the
faint hope of eating iced butterscotch out of them again.

Sometimes I open the suitcase and stare at it for hours.
In the end, I throw out a few things, but always add more
in return.

The suitcase with its thick brown stains stays under my bed,
a place from where it is always visible but not quite reachable.
Its lock has long broken, so I hold it shut with an old orange
shawl. People walk in and out of my room all the time. Some
of them stare at it and move on. But a few pause and stop
altogether. And ask me, with a curving smile and a knowing
glint in their eyes, what I keep hidden for so long.

Sometimes I nod and smile and talk about the world outside.
Sometimes I chew my lips and look at the latest chip in my nail.

Sometimes I look them in the eye and tell them the truth:
That I keep everything stuffed inside, ready to carry if I run
away at a moment's notice. Towards a journey I know I'll one
day escape to.

A journey that will want and take all of me.

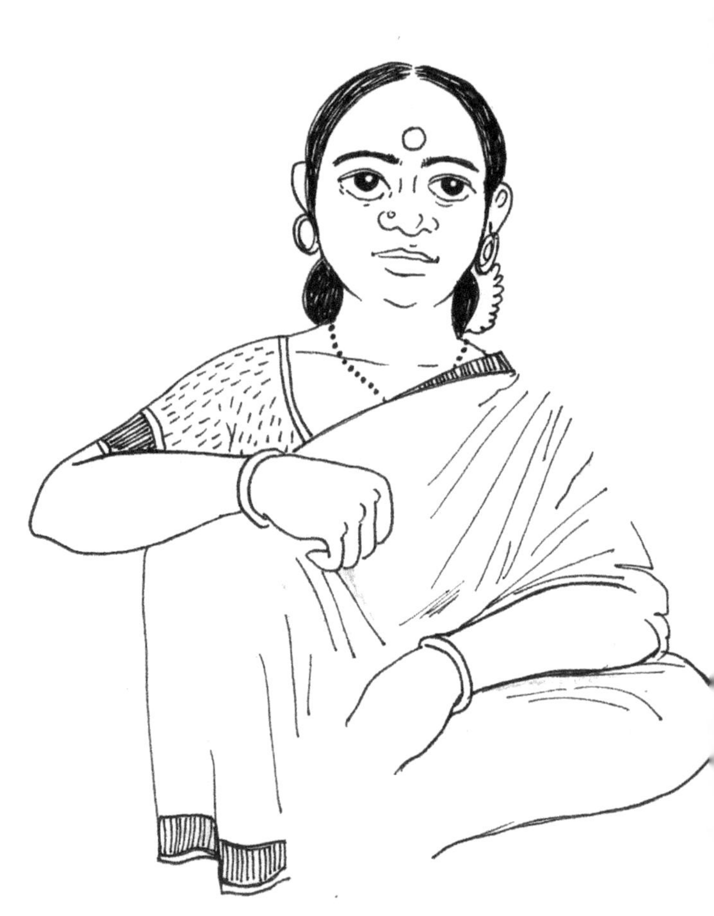

Rasmalai

Long ago, I lived in a place where no one spoke my language or nothing bore any resemblance to home. I used to walk in a place where the floors were inlaid with smooth red stones.

This place had crowded shops on either side of its narrow path. Shops with white umbrellas and slanted blue roofs. They sold clips with butterfly wings and necklaces of seashells. Clothes too expensive to buy, and artists who painted colourful elephants on my nails.

I have walked there too many times. With serene girls who weaved their arms through mine and a boy in a black shirt who couldn't wipe away his stagnant smile.

Once it was raining heavily and I had to take shelter under one of their roofs. The people around me appeared transfixed by the droplets of rain that formed dark patterns on the red floor but remained totally oblivious to everything else that was around.

Nobody grew still like I did on hearing the sudden cry of a woman behind me. It wasn't the voice itself that suddenly made my heart grow heavy. Neither was it the fact that she was shouting on top of her voice.

She was angry. Screaming in a language I knew. A language that I had never heard anyone speak in all the time I'd lived there.

She was shouting in Tamil.

My palms began to sweat, and my fingers followed suit with their slow shiver.

I quickly looked back to find a large woman with a round red bindi right between her brows. Her thick hair was plaited tight, embroidered with a hint of silver. She was wearing an old red saree, and gently blowing the froth from her wooden cup of milk. Sitting behind a counter, she kept shouting along with the patter of the rain. At the thin, wound-up man who stood behind a pot, stirring it, and at any customer who dared to stand too close to her countertop with their dripping clothes and elbows.

The countertop itself was cluttered with silver bowls of all shapes and sizes. Tiny wooden spoons were arranged in small clusters beside them.

The tops of the bowls shimmered with a soft golden glow. Looking closer, I found that they were filled to the brim with bright yellow rasmalai. Groups of two floated at the top within a thick encasing of milk, nuts, and cream. Tiny drops of water collected on the rims and bottoms of the bowls. They had been in the fridge until they were brought out as an offering to the rain.

I forgot how long I had been standing under the gush of rainwater that slid down from the roof. My clothes were soaked and I kept my distance from her bowls.

Every few minutes she dictated another volley of sharp orders at the men making her cakes of rasmalai. Now and then she

also paused to blow away the froth from her cup of milk, but
never took a sip. I listened to her words even after they lost
their meaning. Her voice was strong and loud, filling me with the
wild textures and familiar smells from home. Things I had long
forgotten to feel or remember.

The rain stopped and the people emerged, milling around once
again. Jumping past the muddy puddles, they continued to plead
and bargain and struggle. I sat down at one of the nearby tables,
on a creaky wet chair. My hair had long lost the fluff I set out with
and was now plastered to my arms like overcooked noodles.

Her rough words in their rugged Tamil accent kept finding me
even as the street grew much busier. Every time I heard them,
I stole a glance at her countertop which was the only thing now
visible to me in the crowd. And each time I found myself watching
the saffron add a red glow to the chilled rasmalai and shine under
the new sun.

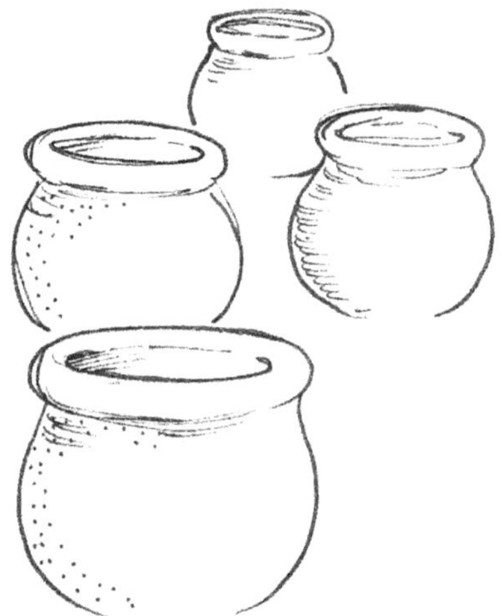

Lemons and Leaves

Your yellow shawl with its tiny green dots.
They catch my eyes first
in a metro crammed with workers
from the end of their day.
With what seems like hundreds of
chattering, wordless women
it is you my eyes are unable to move past.

A sparkling green kurti and a lemon-yellow pant
that widens like a bell at the hem.
Your short black hair held together
in a ponytail that has long since lost
its firmness and is now falling loose,
covering the gold drops on your ears
and the sleeves of your dress.

You are clutching your brown paper bag too hard,
filled with pieces of silk you had hurriedly stuffed in.
Muted reds and pinks, dazzling teals and peacock blue
too incongruous and spilling out,
threatening to slip out of your control
each time you try to push them back in,
deeper than before.

I watch you exit through the doors
with a stumble and a hand flying out
to steady yourself against the world.
You've flawlessly buried yourself under
thick layers of make-up and still
your eyes manage to give it all away.
Looking down, refusing to meet anyone else's.
They are smudged with short black streaks
and shimmer wet under the silent metro lights.

I hope that someone is waiting outside
to kiss your hands, hold you close
till that hard-set expression
thaws and gives way
to what you really want to say.

Or maybe the person or place
you are heading towards is
what is making you cry
and feel the need to stop those
tears from touching the planes
of your glittering cheek.

Maybe none of the above
are true.
And I am just another
stranger
quietly judging you.

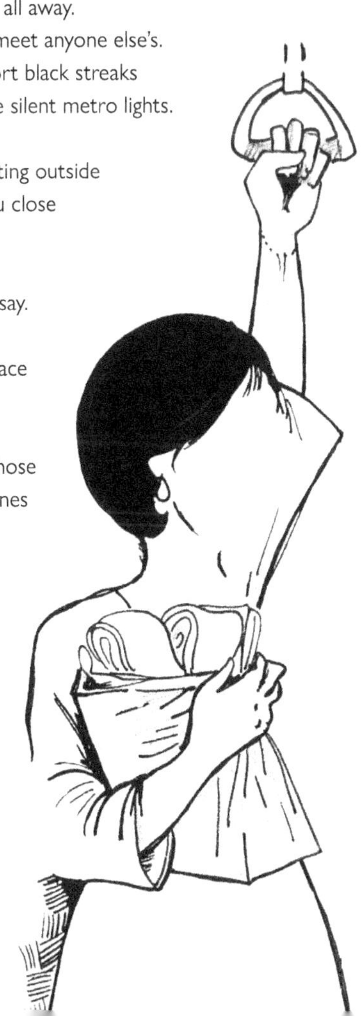

You've probably come from a tiring rehearsal
or a party that was equally exhausting.
Empty and drained at the end of the day
waiting to get back
to the cold confines of your bed.
Just like me.

Whatever it is about you,
one of the many commuters
I come across every night during a busy week,
I can't stop imagining.

What is your story?

Where will you go once you walk out of this greasy station?

The doors glide shut as you walk away.
I lean my head against a warm windowpane
and keep thinking about your receding shadow
long after you are gone.

Parotta

It is 4 am. The food in front of me has long since gone cold. I look at the brown lump, a tangled mess of thinned out gravy, obscure vegetables, and pieces of the hardest parotta I have ever had.

The whole of Delhi is plunged in a deathly cold. In one of its acrimonious corners, I remain awake. My table light, the only means through which I can see the misery on this plate. Home is a thousand miles away as usual and it is time I give up this useless pursuit. This long and disillusioning chase. The desperation to taste the perfect parotta, despite being far away from home.

I think of Madurai. This time it's the night streets and the open stoves that come to mind.

The million times I roamed its lanes, late at night with newly arrived relatives, praying that at least one mess was open.

The feverish delight of finding one.

The flickering beam of light that leads down shady passages before you can get inside. To the hall with grimy plastic tables and broken chairs grouped together for the customers to sit on.

There are no expectations one could have regarding who they would find eating in a mess at that hour. Sometimes it was a bunch of people I knew from school who I didn't think about except when I scrolled past a random post on Instagram. We would smile at each other with vague recognition and turn away to focus on the food.

Other times, it was a group of buoyant young men, loud and reckless with their laughter, likely harmless, in their own corner. Nevertheless, I pick a chair that is far from their line of visibility, ensuring I never have to catch their eye.

The air is thick with smoke and the aroma of spiced meat that I don't bother to distinguish, being vegetarian.

Yet, I carve myself a place. Between plain gravies and basic biryani rice. Ignoring the assorted masalas with meats, arranged in tiny silver bowls, ready to be refilled at a wanting cue.

Excited eyes constantly look over to the large open stove at the entrance that is dotted with snowballs of infantile parotta. The guy behind it, crowned the parotta master, solely helming the whole process. Continuous beads of sweat trickle down his brown arms and shoulders as he flicks and beats the next ball of maida for the thousandth customer of the day.

Nothing can ever replicate that magic of crafting such a parotta, tearing it into chunks and watching it soak up gravy into its multiple layers before each bite.

I look at the sad replica in front of me. It has been four hours since I began eating this hard mound, which had claimed to be an authentic south Indian parotta.

I hear the cat claw against my door, desperate to jump in and inspect the food. I gather the whole of my long-drawn out dinner and stack it on my dish.

Maybe at least one of us can sleep with a satisfied stomach tonight.

I open my door and place the silver plate outside.

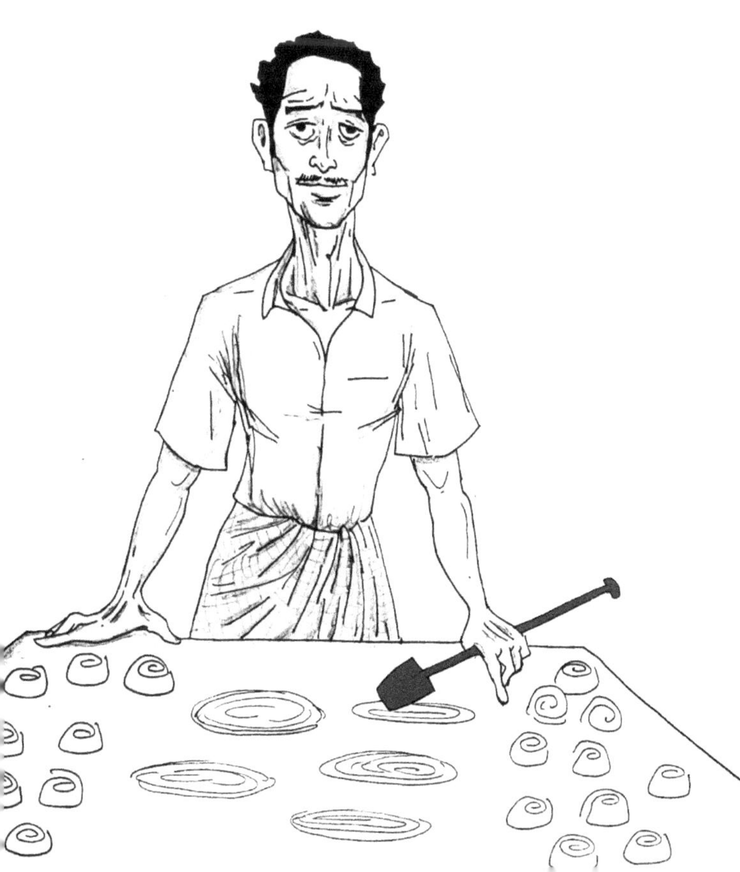

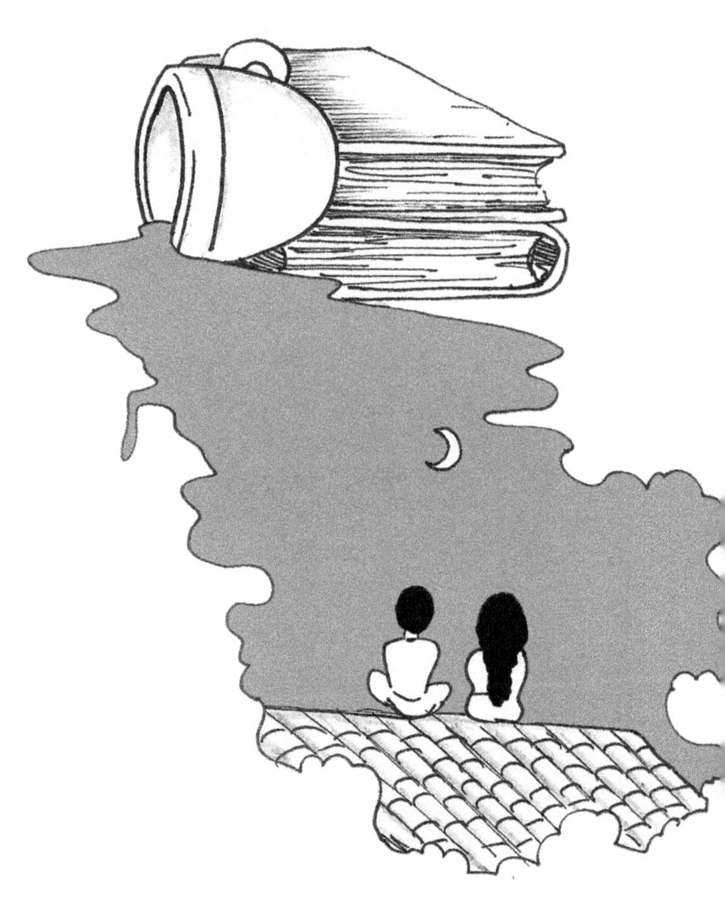

Friend of the Night

I don't really know if I should call her a friend.

Her hair is cut short. Each wisp curling into black streaks
against her cheek.

She likes purple lipstick and wears expensive black shirts.
She doesn't smile or talk out of turn, and walks with girls like
her. We don't message each other on birthdays or celebrate
each other's successes.

By daylight, nobody even knows if we talk or exchange a nod.
But when dusk falls, she climbs over my creaky gate in a new
pair of jeans, a tattered book clutched tight.

We sit on top of the terrace, so high up in the sky that the stars
we find there are completely different from those everyone else
can see. Heads against the wet stone wall, we look up at the
rising moon and pretend like nothing is odd.

Her fingers press hard against the spine of the book before
she breaks the silence with an outburst that is new every time.
"I don't want to read anymore." Her voice is a low whisper
while her eyes take in the blinking speck of a plane high up
in the night sky.

I think of the three books that have wrung out her heart the
past week and smile. The tips of my toes are covered by my faded
skirt. I feel my pink shawl flutter in the wind.

"Which one of them died this time?" I ask.

There is a slight slumber in the air before the words erupt,
carrying our voices to worlds far away from the little city she
and I know. Books we read years ago but still carry around, the
dimly lit library in our school, and the alternate realities that could
never happen in the stories we know.

We compose our own lores with characters we both love.
Talk and talk about the mistakes the author made. How many
times we shut a book, smiling about the line we just read.
Novels we exchange and never return.

Bookmarks we hoard and compare and secretly covet.
Dragons we hope to fly away with. The strange men in fiction
we fall in love with.

Classics might be better, but are never as sweet as the young
adult fiction we adore. Magical quests filled with doom, dust
fairies studying in schools, and star-crossed lovers beyond
all hope. And deaths that pierce and spring out of the page,
occurring as if it were always meant to be.

Hours and hours go by. Sighing about the brilliant worlds we
will never see, arguing about the unknown morals in the tale,
and building a reality far more real than the one we exist within.
We don't hug or exchange gifts. We never talk about boyfriends

or the way our hearts tingle when we're kissed. We don't grow close and barely know anything about each other beyond the books we read.

When sunlight breaks, she is gone, and we continue with our separate lives. Our eyes don't meet across the hall and she is never the first person I think about when I want someone to catch my fall.

But sometimes, when the sun is too bright and I find myself sitting away from everyone, leaning against the grassy bark of a tree, I open another book with a story both new and old. Turning its crusted pages while reading the same beloved lines, my mind drifts to her, my dear friend of the night, and I wonder what she thinks of it all.

aster

white stars vanish under a cherry nut tree
when you first sip frozen chocolate with me.
a thawed heart loops and weaves
our story in the above olive leaves.
standing calm against the red red tree
you talk of a journey through the sea.
of curved clouds in the climb
and lemongrass stalks past their prime.
i lean in as our echoes tense to rhyme.
close your eyes.
i'll kiss you for a dime.

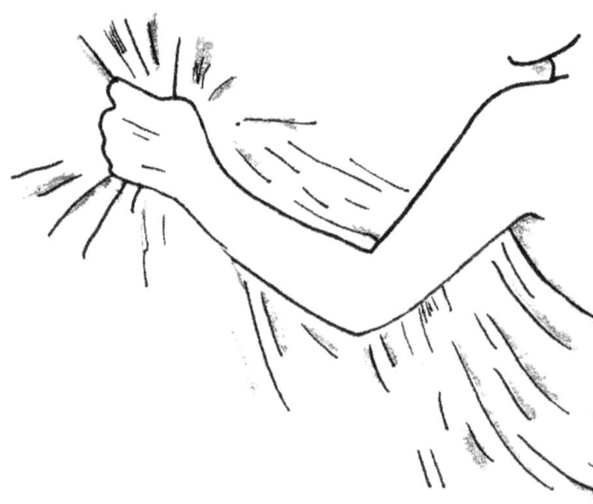

Icicles

I look at my fingertips,
blue-smeared half-moons
imprinted deep.
I held the pen
too long today.
The dull notebook paper
stays still,
bearing blotches and strikes.
A scratch here
and several more there.
The words are quiet.
They don't budge.
They don't breathe
or call out to each other.

I have tried
too hard to mend
these words.
To polish the coarse refrains,
tighten the images that burst
around the corners
of a simile
and fix the meter
you said ran askew.
I couldn't stop trying.
Not until the verses

crammed to fit a single page
And formed a lull and a lilt
as they rolled through your mind
and made you smile.

I had forgotten
the world behind the words.
I had forgotten
that they were once real.
The scars that burned
in pits of blood.
Blood that flowed
down my legs
and left lingering shades of pain.
The raw stench of loss
borne through starless skies.

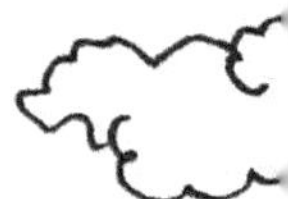

You aren't aware of them.

When your eyes
flick past their carcasses
deeply frozen
crimped and cut
to fit the scented pages
of the book you bought fresh.

There was a time
none of this
could be shielded
or shrunk
to fit the foliage of words.

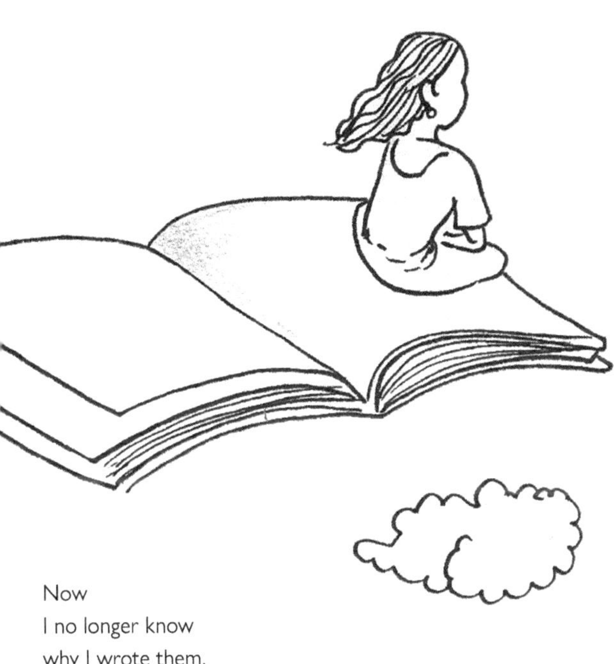

Now
I no longer know
why I wrote them.

These faded lines
had once filled me
like the bubbling rays
of an early dawn.
The warmth I could only find
when holding brown paper bags
of fresh bread loaves
from the baker down the street.
And tracing my fingers
against the brown spots and blisters
of books that were read
and re-read
long long before me.

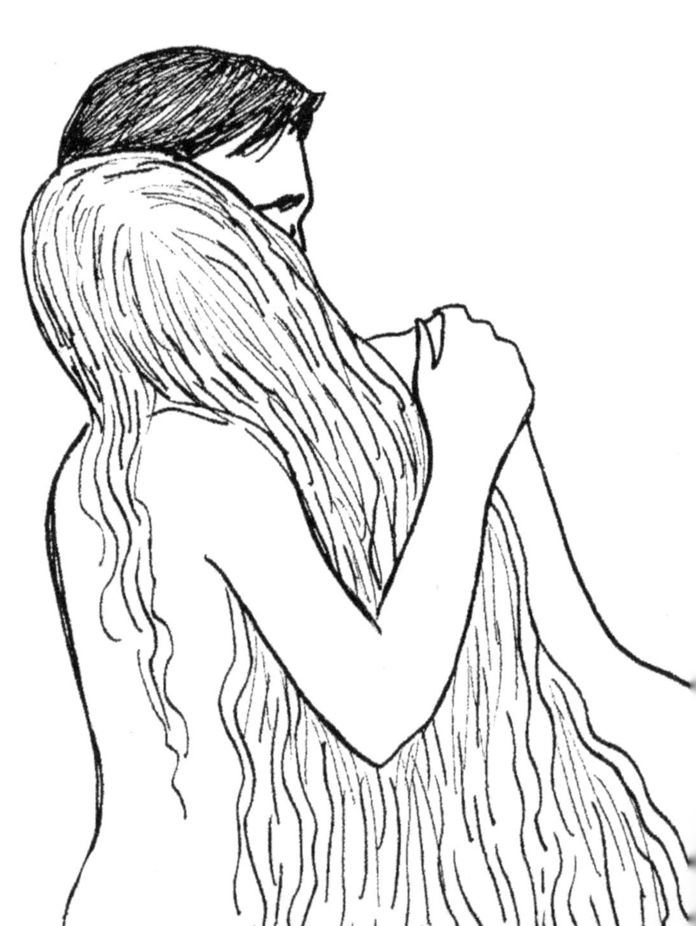

aurora

I think of you between absent breakfasts in the morning
and a gentle craving for milk
with sugared froth that slowly builds during the day.
sometimes it strikes sharp, just a
quick terrible ache.
other times I wait, curious,
wondering which one of them will hit first.

it is always those cheap hotel rooms.
the cramped streets below crowded with people
trickling out to the world in bored flashy colours.
the hollow corridors that twist and twirl
before ending in a splatter of cubical rooms
and how I follow you through them to ours,
your shirt clutched tight between my shivering fingers,
hoping that this wouldn't be the
last time.
the strange little room.
my eyes tracing down
every stain and spot
on the yellowed walls and
floors carpeted in patches.
the strange little room
and how it always changes in the end;
into a home with its familiar broken tiles,
jagged mirrors and loose bed springs.

meals of tea and hot chocolate,
steaming in tall purple cups
trailing into the bed
staining those white bedsheets in two warm puddles
of light and burnished brown
before they merge into one.
plastic boxes with fries and salt shaken to opposite corners
and you and me bent over the white container with leftover gravy
fingers working as a team
hunting for stray baby corn without words.
fights hit the hard limits of fury
thaws and cracks into unstoppable tears
hours and hours of unfilled silence
long showers in a bathroom that barely fits one
learning to stroke your damp cheek
in ways you didn't think you liked.
your hands in my wet hair
drying it with the towel we share
the water forming shapeless drops on your chest.

when we lie down naked under the sheets
smelling strong of pink hotel soap
I can feel you think.
is this an inescapable cage we have woven around us
or a cradle of the softest silk
that is meant to be?

the lanes beyond the half-open windows,
are struck by flashes of heavy downpour.
fill up deep with rain water
and dries under a sudden scorching sun.

the crowded streets
shelved into rows of green chairs and huge speakers
with a continuum of blaring chants.
the other side of the window however is laced with
moth-eaten curtains
where reality is muted to a background screen.
clothes and bags strewn all over the bed and floor.
we lie tangled in between, the days and nights merging into
an endless shard of time. stomachs untucked and bare.
kissing slowly, every long scar that traces your body.

we could have been in landour's peaks
with red tinted cheeks and windswept hair
sitting outside
their corner cafes and spotted outdoor umbrellas
or in the giant villas that dot the goan coast
amidst the melodrama of their lapping waves
bunched up all night
talking by the fireplace.

but every time I think of you,
this will be the first thing I remember:

the cheap hotel rooms.

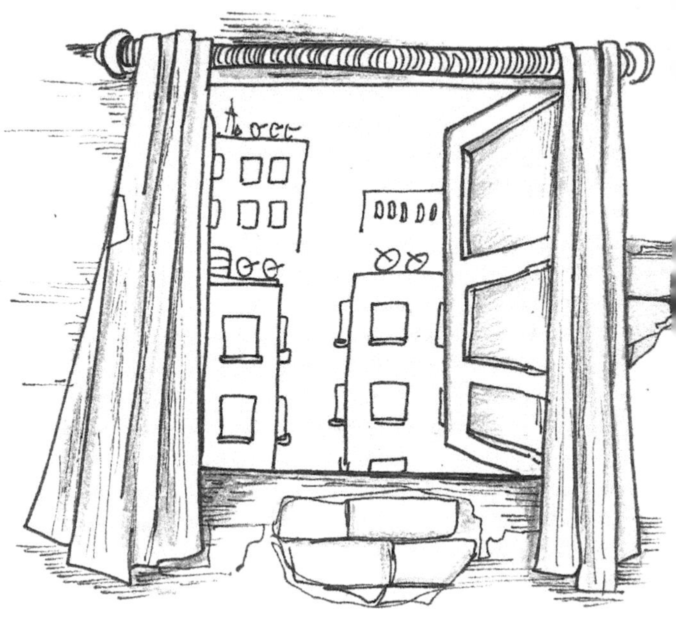

Cinderella Night

She walks alone on the road leading home. It is mostly empty
at this early hour except for a few roadside stalls opening up,
with morning biscuits and simmering pots of tea.

A small smile flickers on her lips.

Her eyes strain to look beyond the clump of stones she kicks
away from her path.

Caught up in the slow stream of images in her mind, she doesn't
really care to look at the world waking up around her.

Her hair is mussed and sticks to the side of her face as she
makes her way through the early morning chill. The little bindi
she applied last evening with a brush dipped in black mascara held
on through the night, before fading away until it left no more than
a small curve on her sticky forehead. Her lips are dry and crusted
with stubborn shades of lipstick and her cheeks carry the creases
of the hotel bed sheets she could never sleep in.

She tries to stifle a low yawn and keeps trudging forward in
her green dress. The dress hugged her close last night, framing
her from neck to knee and swishing every way she wanted it to.
She finds herself wondering how the same dress which lit her
up last night can now hang, lovelorn and dull, despite the early
embers of the morning sun.

She smiles as if there is nobody around. Walks like she has all the time to reach where she's going. She thinks of his fingers reaching over the table and wiping off the cheese from the corners of her lips. She thinks of his eyes and the way they bore into hers as he twirled his fork in the pasta, mixing the corn and olives.

A sudden shiver starts from the tips of her bare toes.

She remembers him holding her close under the sheets, their skin blazing against each other and their clothes in a wanton pile by the bed. She thinks of him in his red and black sweater, suitcases packed and ready to fly back home, even before she was awake. His last hug. Their last touch. The final smile. Hesitant. Cool. Perfunctory. Never as warm as before, no longer blazing.

She pauses for a moment. She will always be a tiny piece of his vacation on lands fascinating for their unfamiliarity.

But he is to her, an incorrigible tale of adventure.

She starts walking again. Quicker than before. Wanting to get away from the fresh morning air and back to the dampness of her flat. She doesn't look at the world that is gently nudged awake as the morning rays grow brighter. She doesn't hear the clink of the milk bottles that wait outside her house, fresh with froth and the thickest of creams.

She heaves a sigh of relief as she opens the door. The couch is flowing with biscuit crumbs, wrappers, and oil-tinged pizza boxes from the past week. Her clothes lie in a knotted clump beside the couch; laundered ones entangled with everything she had thrown around while trying to find an outfit for the previous day. The paint on the walls, once a creamy white, has begun to peel again, exposing the cracks and craters in the cement it conceals. The air smells like cat litter and there is also the cloying scent of the broken perfume bottles on her windowsills.

She removes her heels and rubs the red marks they left on her feet.

Sighing deeply, she closes her eyes for a minute and thinks about her empty fridge and unattended emails.

She walks over to her window and pushes away the broken bottles of fragrance. The sun lights up her creased, tired skin with a golden sheen. For a moment she looks luminous in her leftover lipstick and sleep riddled face. As if realizing this, she shuts her curtains. Then sneezes in rapid succession at the cloud of dust they release. Wiping her nose on the sleeve of her dress, she walks to her bed. The grey dimness veils the seeping sunlight of the day.

Her blankets are coiled just the way she left them. Picking the sheets up, she makes a half-hearted attempt at dusting them down before slipping beneath. She draws her knees close to her chest and holds the pillow under her head. She runs a hand across her cheek to push away all the hair sticking to her face and sniffs once. Then twice as her eyes begin to close.

And in the moment before she falls asleep, she thinks of the ache between her legs and the emptiness in her chest.

embers

the first day after I knew you'd left
I pretended that I hadn't seen or heard anything
and fell back asleep

the second day, I read over and over again
everything we'd texted last
a few tears slipped from my unsure eyes
and I never left the bed

the day after that, I thought of you sitting
outside my place with a warm sweater
milkshakes in paper cups and your last bar of chocolate
I should have said something unexpected
something that made you think
and linger a lot longer than you did

five days later, I shuddered all over
still frozen in the barrenness of my bed
wondering if it was the intensity of your spinning thoughts
or the complete blankness of them
that drove you to leave so quick,
so sudden. with no warning and every plan left hanging.

after I lost count of the days
the heaviness had clawed its dry pits
all over my breath and thought

every song I now listen to
is another song
I will never hear you sing for me
every new book I try to read
is another story you will never know

I wish you had left your old underlined novels
the books you were meant to return
or at least the tales you made me bookmark

to know what to expect
to tell me what to do

because until you
death was always a cold draught
striking places that were never mine

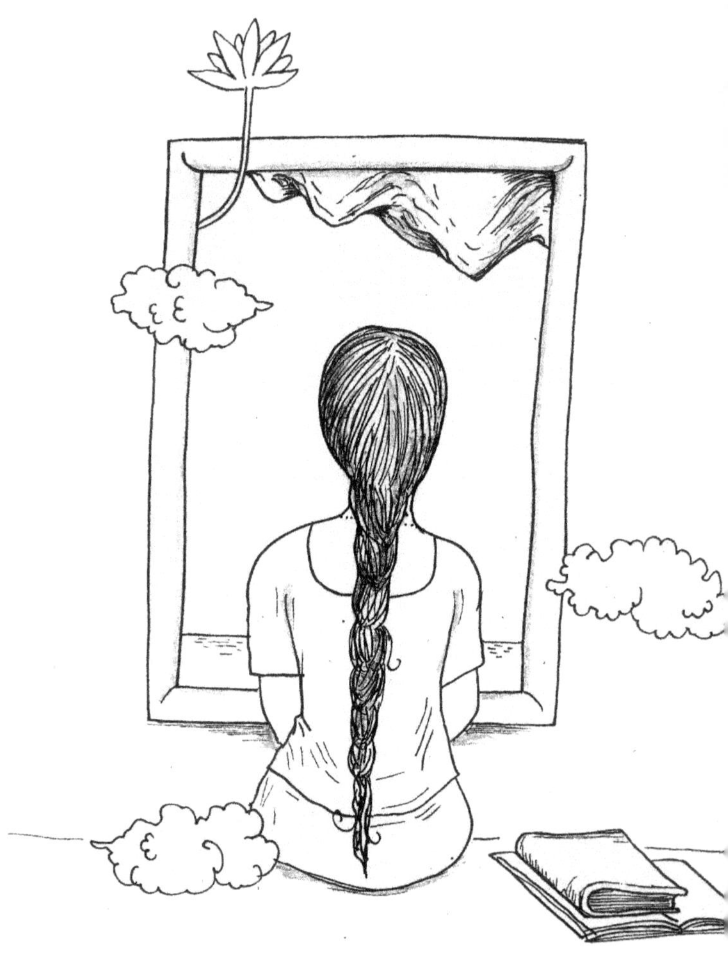

To the girl I dream about

Sometimes you are more real than I am. You are powerful. More powerful than I am. And more vulnerable than I can ever imagine myself to be in my waking and walking moments. There is a flutter in my heart and a flicker in my eyes when I think about you. I live in a reality that's more muted than yours. I'm careful about what I see, what I listen to and what I allow myself to think. I know I must not dwell close to certain things. Things that still blaze and froth, waiting to upturn and rain chaos upon the careful clutter of my mind. I usually keep them away during the day. Ignore them. Close my eyes. Take a deep breath. And pretend they do not exist. Hence my days do not get too sharp or vivid. Blunt around the edges. A watered-down version of yours.

When it is your time, there is no place to hide. You live through everything I am too scared to feel. You can't outrun things the way I do. You kick, crawl, cry and try to breathe in a place that smothers you all night. I watch your eyes widen in shock. I look at your hair curling against the shivering skin on your arms. I feel every shaking breath you struggle to take. I wish I can reach you. Take your greased cheek between the palm of my two hands, press your forehead to mine and whisper that it will be okay in a few more hours as soon as the daylight dawns. But you know I can't. The invisible gauze that keeps us apart never weakens, no matter what. You are on the other side of reality and I am here. I can only watch. Keep watching all my life.

Dear You. The girl of my dreams. I try hard every day. And hope. Hope that I can keep you safe. I drench myself in fairy tales and wish that you will be okay. Holding a warm hand, looking into a pair of affectionate eyes, reading another book and waiting for more chocolate pastries. I try to do everything we love. Sometimes it makes your life better. You are okay for a few days. I know this because I see you in my favourite place during those times. A place that felt more like home than home itself. I find you in the library built inside my school.

One I haven't seen in years and years but somehow you still remember in perfect detail. You walk through the closed doors, grazing the tips of your fingers on the dusty covers of all those books. You stop near the glass windows at the back and look out at the endless grounds. The breeze cradles your nose and the crusty edges of your lips. The library is always dimly lit. Sometimes you are naked as you walk through it. The waning sunlight changes into shimmers of gold and brown as it touches the bareness of your skin. You look radiant then. Beautiful in a place you thrive the most. At that moment, I never remember the last time I looked like you.

But soon everything shakes apart. Before you are pulled into the lure of what I avoid, we end up somewhere blank and weird. Something we never understand. Once I saw you swaddled in a heavy saree of cream and silk. You had diamonds on your ears and circles of gold around your neck and wrist. There were candles around. Candles which laced the air with scents of warm vanilla sugar and the incense from my home. Your hair was in a thick long braid. I looked at the maroon where your hair divides and the fresh rings on your toes. You were a bride and I couldn't help but smile. That wasn't a bad place for you to be.

Then the air turned putrid and stank of rotten eggs. The jasmine in your hair wrinkled and withered, turning a sickly shade of grey. I knew what was coming. You never realized that you were being sucked back in until you were already deep inside. You are innocent every time.

Usually, there is anger in the air. Dead friends waiting to throttle you from somewhere. People touch you here. Men and women. Men I know and women I trust. They touch you often. You never open your mouth. They fondle and prod. Touch and tweak. Sometimes stab. You stand mute. Trying to run fast with a pair of legs in deep slumber. You never outrun them all. I beat through the gauze, begging for it to open. Hoping to save you once and for all. When nothing works, I try to shut my eyes to not see any of it again. There is silence.

You never scream or shout. The anger smoulders within you, slowly charring all of you. The quietness rumbles from you. I see you beaten. I see you drilled. I know how you look covered in blood. You sit and take it all. The people around you grovel and laugh. Stamping their feet and dancing along. But somehow your silence triumphs them all. Battered and bruised, I ask you. Shout at you. Why don't you ever talk or say what you want? Why don't you scream or spit or plunge a dagger into their hearts?

You look at me from afar and a smile so serene breaks across your wounded face. You point at me again and again. Of course,

I understand what you are trying to say. How can you conjure speech and sound when it is me that's the wordless one?

You should know this. When I wake up with pits of black around my eyes and a palette of things I can't feel, somehow I still do not let go of you. You are there in me. Still living in my mind and heart. Riding dragons, running barefoot and living in a world of colours. A world that stays within my mind and is completely different from what's outside of it. You live there. Doing things I never can.

To smooth the sharpness of your life, I like to pretend that the nightmares are just a giant work of fiction. I remember the best part of my dreams. Where I glide over water, walk among books and kiss without fear. I pretend that they are nothing more than beautiful worlds waiting to be written. Because when I write, you and I are no longer different. We become one and soar through mountains and oceans of words. You become me. And I become you.

And when I don't write, I wonder. What if you are who I truly am? Feeling every inch of the pain and every freckle of joy. What if you are who I am supposed to be? What if I am just a weak hint of who you really are with all your intensity?

What if you aren't just smothered in my night dreams? What if I am doing it too? Even while I am awake? Stifling and hiding you from the world, ignoring all your shoves and struggles to break through me. Because most times I feel like I sleep through life and live in my dreams.

And at the end of the day, it is always you I write about, never me.

Vellichor

The window is closed. I look at everything that is outside.
There is the sun and the heat from it. The trees without leaves.
The way they gently sway. There is the wind rushing past buildings
and against the wings of flighty birds. The occasional car and
the traces of last night's snow. Your footsteps when you walked
in yesterday. The dusty handprints on the window pane.

I can hear the silent murmur of a radio from the market down
the street. It makes me think of busy airports, and takeaways with
chocolate fudge cakes and sweetened coffee.

The sun is still overhead. My forehead is pressed to the window.
You are sitting at the table behind me. Looking up things on your
phone and sighing every time you get something right. There is an
orange mug beside you. With a grey teddy bear and green leaves
painted on its surface. A slow spoon mixing the milk with the
excessive sugar in it.

The page next to me is empty. It does not bother me much
right now. The pen has rolled off the bed and I don't look for it
like I usually do. There are tiny patterns of dust and something
else on the window, and I think about how I often do not know
the words to describe many things I see or feel. The prints on
the window for instance. How else do I describe those shapes
and swirls if not a pattern? What else can I see but dust marks
I hadn't remembered to wipe?

It has been a few minutes and my mind already tingles to look for
my phone. Look at it to see if there is a message from you. When
you are right there next to me, stirring the milk and lost in your
world of thoughts. I know I shouldn't call out to you. Not right
now. You need to be lost. And I need to be here. Looking at the
wind outside whose touch I can't feel. The sun whose warmth
barely reaches my toes. And cars and people who I can't hear
or reach out to.

There are words I sometimes struggle to remember. I catch a
slight whiff of their presence but nothing more. The harder I try
to reach out to them, the faster they disappear. Will I want to
find my pen if I remember what I wanted to write? Will this page
be filled if I could get down more than a word or two at one go?

Will all these thoughts stop if I turn away from the window?

I want to turn to you. Shake you from your reverie. And ask
if you sometimes feel nostalgic for a moment while still in it.
If you think about something that is happening in terms of how
it will feel many years from now. I want to know if the evening
lights inside a landing plane makes you think about the tops of
lonely castles and smoky pink walls. If the saltiness that lingers
on the fingertips after a tub of popcorn makes you want to walk
on streets that are unknown. Streets that will take you further
and further away from home.

I want to sit by the bridge tonight and tell you about the time
I watched the leaves fall from a tree that stood outside the school
my friend studied in. I was very young and waiting for her to get
out of class. The tree was huge and filled with fresh drops of rain.

The leaves formed a bright green foliage but still fluttered down one after the other. Leaving the tree on its own. It reminded me of an old Agatha Christie book I had just borrowed from the library. One I was very excited to start reading that night.

The school bell rang. My friend walked out after all of her classmates did. We went back home. There were board games with mermaids, strawberry candies and rainbow-coloured cakes before she left. I began reading the book after. A book whose name I don't remember. In fact, everything I know from that day is filled with a blank cloud of haze. Everything but those few moments when I watched those leaves fall. Moments I would have never thought about if not for you.

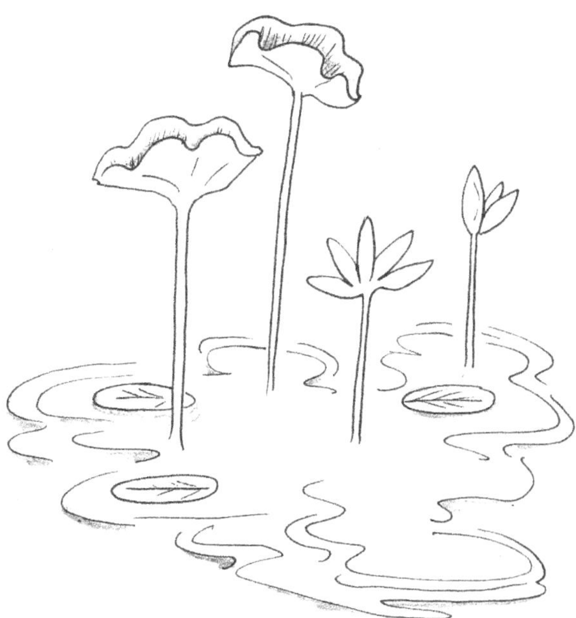

I want to go to the bridge tonight and tell you how it actually
felt when I ran away from people and could never feel safe until
I was by myself. That it wasn't just anxiety, but anger that pushed
me away from real voices to the comfort of heavy sheets. Anger
that I cannot talk about. Anger that has never once left my head
in the past years, and the anger that I need to be extremely
careful about.

I think of radios playing over market aisles and how that conjures
pictures of you and me in airports to countries and worlds
nobody knows about. I look past the window again. The world
appears muted in its ways and blurred no matter how many
times I clear my mind. The window is dusty and thick, keeping
the outside far away like it should.

I look at you again and this time don't look away. I do not think
about all the words that should have been on my mind.

There are shadows behind my eyes. Shadows that sometimes
stretch past where they are allowed to be and enter the room
with you and me.

I look at you and am reminded of the books I need to pick up
from the library and of tears I never knew were there.

nefelibata

find me by the lake
beyond the curl of clouds
crouched in the garden
of wheat and purple maize.

the lake stands still
pulsing with echoes of tales
you don't know the shape of.
it lives. it breathes.
houses feelings more potent
than you or me.

sit with your legs folded
on the cracked wooden plank
that drops at the edge
into the damp secrets below.

talk. talk slow. talk loud.
talk the way I whisper into your ear.
let your voice caress the water's surface
where images begin to flit.

dark green creepers in a jungle
lonely sheep in a farm
a throbbing yellow sky
they keep moving faster with your voice.

there is a sudden whirl
in the middle of the lake
don't let your voice quiver
stand up and walk straight
to the edge of the plank
and meet what you came for.

the children of the lake
moonstones for eyes
built with a shimmer of soft gray
glide towards you
from the center of the swirl.

they talk back
in slow silent whispers.
hold your hand.

close your eyes.

they soak your words
the tremor in your voice
they sing tales
that will take you home
no matter where you are.

come sit by my side
near the lake in the garden
and tell me everything.

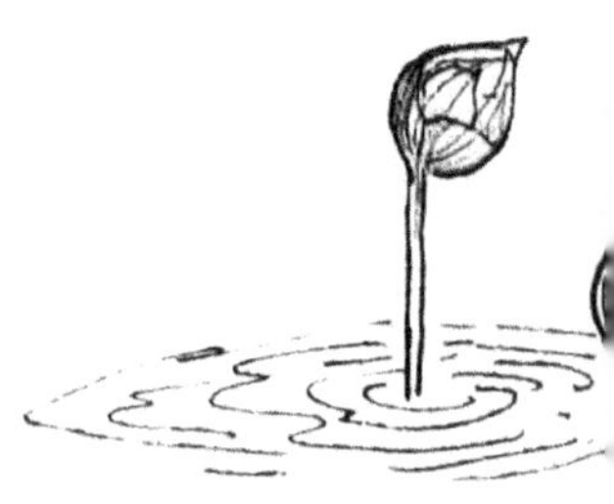

it doesn't matter
the language or tone
or who you are.

the lake will listen.
talk.

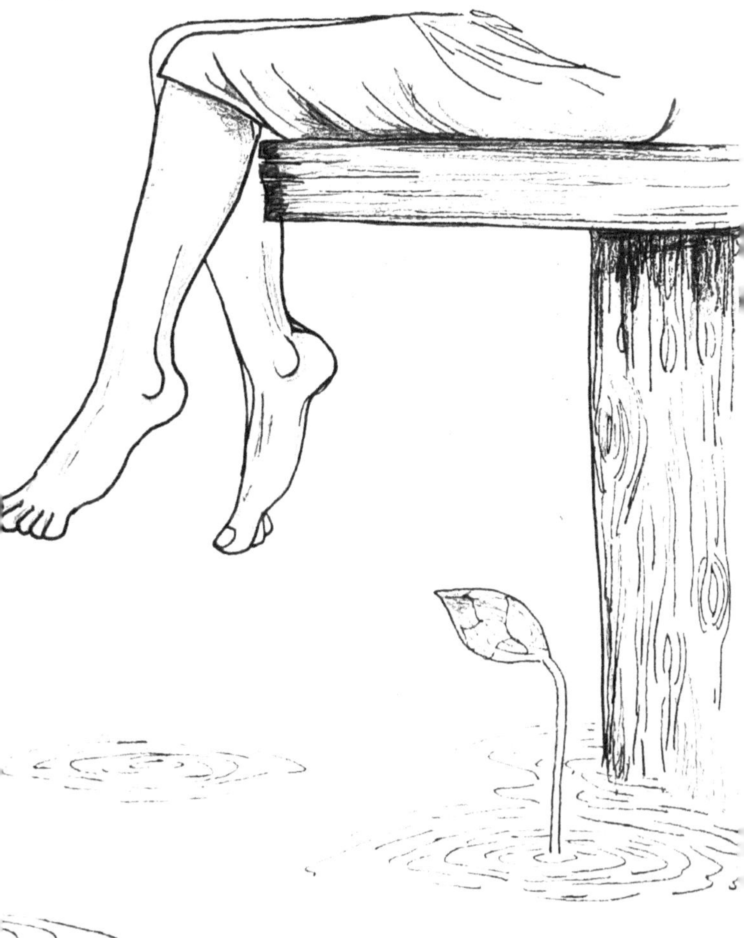

About the author

Hariny grew up amidst the ancient temples in the city of
Madurai in Tamil Nadu. Her work has been published in the
Verse of Silence, the *Intersect Journal* and The Open Culture
Collective. Her first book, *the dictionary of flowers* is set in
India and talks about a young woman learning and unlearning
the stories she grew up with. She lives in London and can
be found lost between the pages of hardcovers or intensely
focused on pots of boiling rice.

About the illustrator

Rohit Bhasi is a Bangalore based illustrator and graphic designer.
His work is a personal interpretation of the various myths, tales
and belief systems that populate his part of the world. He is
also fascinated by the human body and its evolving potential
for creation, beauty and storytelling. His work can be seen
on instagram and facebook under the name 'indigoranges'.

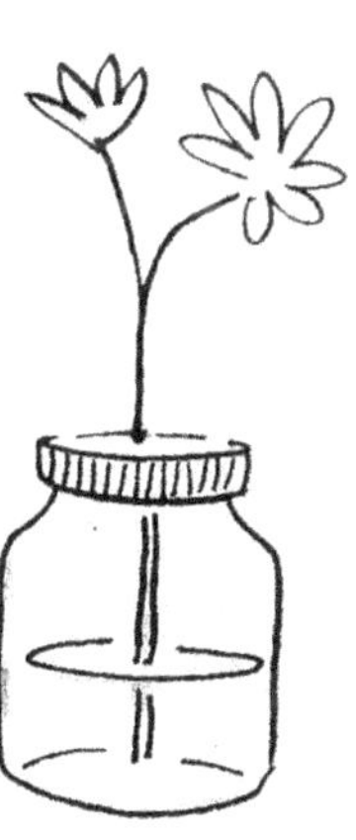